CYRUS THE GREAT: A LIFE IN ONE VOLUME

GOLU KUMAR

Contents

CHAPTER ONE

Tonight, I want to talk to you about one of those ancient autocratic empires, which were always the oldest forms of known civilization. If I were to play the cynic or the mountebank, I would pick a corrupt and effete despotism that had already succumbed to decay and had become weak and ridiculous—as did the Roman and then the Byzantine Empire—and, after making fun of the old order, declare: "See what a superior people you are now—how impossible is anything so base and so absurd as went on, even in despotic France before the Revolution of 1793." Thank God, that would generally be the case, so why mention it again?

Let us keep our scorn for our weaknesses, our blame for our sins, certain that we shall gain more instruction, though not more amusement, by hunting out the good which is in anything than by hunting out its evil. I have chosen, not the worst, but the best despotism which I could find in history, founded and ruled by a truly heroic personage, one whose name has become a proverb and a legend, that so I might lift your minds, even by the contemplation of an old Eastern empire, to see that it, too, could be a work and ordinance of God, and its hero the servant of the Lord. For we are almost bound to call Cyrus, the founder of the Persian Empire, by this august title for two reasons--First, because the Hebrew Scriptures call him so; the next, because he proved himself to be such by his actions and their consequences--at least in the eyes of those who believe, as I do, in a far-seeing and far-reaching Providence, by which all human history is

Bound by gold chains unto the throne of God.

His work was very different from any that needs to be done, or can be done, these days. But while we thank God that such work is now as unnecessary as impossible; we may thank God likewise that, when such work was necessary and possible, a man was raised to do it: and to do it, as all accounts assert, better, perhaps, than it had ever been done before or since.

True, the old conquerors, who absorbed nation after nation, tribe after tribe, and founded empires on their ruins, are now, I trust, about to be replaced, throughout the world, as here and in Britain at home, by free self-governed peoples:

The old order changeth, giving place to the new;
And God fulfills Himself in many ways,
Lest one good custom should corrupt the world.

And that custom of conquest and empire and transplantation did more than once corrupt the world. And yet in it, too, God may have more than once fulfilled His designs, as He did, if Scripture is to be believed, in Cyrus, well surnamed the Great, the founder of the Persian Empire some 2400 years ago. For these empires, it must be remembered, did at least that which the Roman Empire did among a scattered number of savage tribes, or separate little races, hating and murdering each other, speaking different tongues, worshipping different gods, and losing utterly the sense of a common humanity, till they looked on the people who dwelt in the next valley as friends, to be sacrificed, if caught, to their friends at home. Among such these, empires did introduce order, law, common speech, common interest, and the notion of nationality, and humanity. They, as it were, hammered together the fragments of the human race till they had molded them into one. They did it cruelly, clumsily, ill: but was there ever work done on earth, however noble, which was not--alas, alas!--done somewhat ill?

Let me talk to you a little about the old hero. He and his hardy Persians should be especially interesting to us. For in the first does our race, the Aryan race, appear in authentic history. In the first did our race gives promise of being the conquering and civilizing race of the future world. And to the conquests of Cyrus--so strangely are all great times and great movements of the human family linked to each other--to his conquests, humanly speaking, is owing the fact that you are here, and I am speaking to you at this moment.

It is an oft-told story: but so grand a one that I must sketch it for you, however clumsily, once more.

In that mountain province called Farsistan, north-east of what we now call Persia, the dwelling-place of the Persians, there dwelt, in the sixth and seventh centuries before Christ, a hardy tribe, of the purest blood of Iran, a branch of the same race as the Celtic, Teutonic, Greek, and Hindoo, and speaking a tongue akin to theirs. They had wandered thither, say their legends, out of the far north-east, from off some lofty plateau of Central Asia, driven out by the increasing cold, which left them but two mouths of summer to ten of winter.

They despised at first--would that they had despised always!--the luxurious life of the dwellers in the plains, and the effeminate customs of the Medes--a branch of their race who had conquered and intermarried with the Turanian, or Finnish tribes; and adopted much of their creed, as well as of their morals, throughout their vast but short- lived Median Empire. "Soft countries," said Cyrus himself--so runs the tale--"gave birth to small men. No region produced at once delightful fruits and men of a war-like spirit." Letters were to them, probably, then unknown. They borrowed them for years, as they borrowed their art, from Babylonians, Assyrians, and other Semitic nations whom they conquered. From the age of five to that of twenty, their lads were instructed but in two things--to speak the truth and to shoot with the bow. To ride was the third necessary art, introduced, according to Xenophon, after they had descended from their mountain fastnesses to conquer the whole East.

Their creed was simple enough. Ahura Mazda--Ormuzd, as he has been called since--was the one eternal Creator, the source of all light and life and good. He spake his word, and it accomplished the creation of heaven, before the water, before the earth, before the cow, before the tree, before the fire, before man the truthful, before the Devas and beasts of prey, before the whole existing universe; before every good thing created by Ahura Mazda and springing from Truth.

He needed no sacrifices of blood. He was to be worshipped only with prayers, with offerings of the inspiring juice of the now unknown herb Homa, and by the preservation of the sacred fire, which, understand, was not he, but the symbol--as was light and the sun--of the good spirit--of Ahura Mazda. They had no images of the gods, these old Persians; no temples, no altars, so says Herodotus and considered the use of them a sign of folly. They were, as has been well saying of them, the Puritans of the old world. When they descended from their mountain fastnesses, they became the iconoclasts of the old world; and the later

Isaiah, out of the depths of national shame, captivity, and exile, saw in them brother-spirits, the chosen of the Lord, whose hero Cyrus, the Lord was holding by His right hand, till all the foul superstitions and foul effeminacies of the rotten Semitic peoples of the East, and even of Egypt itself, should be crushed, though, alas! only for a while, by men who felt that they had a commission from the God of light and truth and purity, to sweep out all that with the besom of destruction.

But that was a later inspiration. In earlier, and it may be happier, times the duty of the good man was to strive against all evil, disorder, uselessness, and incompetence in their more simple forms. "He, therefore, is a holy man," says Ormuzd in the Zend-Avesta, "who has built a dwelling on the earth, in which he maintains fire, cattle, his wife, his children, and flocks and herds; he who makes the earth produce barley, he who cultivates the fruits of the soil, cultivates purity; he advances the law of Ahura Mazda as much as if he had offered a hundred sacrifices."

To reclaim the waste, to till the land, to make a corner of the earth better than they found it, was to these men to rescue a bit of Ormuzd's world out of the usurped dominion of Ahriman; to rescue it from the spirit of evil and disorder for its rightful owner, the Spirit of Order and of Good.

For they believed in an evil spirit, these old Persians. Evil was not for them a lower form of good. With their intense sense of the difference between right and wrong it could be nothing less than hateful; to be attacked, exterminated, as a personal enemy, till it became to them, at last, impersonate and a person.

Zarathustra, the mystery of evil, weighed heavily on them and their great prophet, Zoroaster--the splendor of gold, as I am told his name signifies--who lived, no man knows clearly when or clearly where, but who lived and lives forever, for his works follow him. He, too, tried to solve for his people the mystery of evil; and if he did not succeed, who has succeeded yet? Warring against Ormuzd, Ahura Mazda, was Ahriman, Angra Mainyus, literally the being of an evil mind, the ill-conditioned being. He was laboring perpetually to spoil the good work of Ormuzd alike in nature and man. He was the cause of the fall of man, the tempter, the author of misery and death; he was eternal and uncreate as Ormuzd was. But that, perhaps, was a corruption of the purer and older Zoroastrian creed. With it, if Ahriman were eternal in the past, he would not be eternal in the future. Somehow, somewhen, somewhere, in the day when three prophets--the increasing light, the increasing truth, and the existing truth--should arise and give to mankind the last three books of the Zend-Avesta, and convert all mankind to the pure creed, then evil should be conquered, the creation becomes pure again, and Ahriman vanish forever; and, meanwhile, every good man was to fight valiantly for Ormuzd, his true lord, against Ahriman and all his works.

Men who held such a creed, and could speak the truth and draw the bow, what might they not do when the hour and the man arrived? They were not a _big_ nation. No; but they were a _great_ nation, even while they were eating barley bread and paying tribute to their conquerors the Medes, in the sterile valleys of Farsistan.

And at last, the hour and the man came. The story is half legendary--differently told by different authors. Herodotus has one tale, Xenophon another. The first, at least, had ample means of information. Astyages is the old shah of the Median Empire, then at the height of its seeming might and splendor and effeminacy. He has married his daughter, Princess Mandane, to Cambyses, seemingly a vassal-king or prince of pure Persian blood. One night the old man is troubled by a dream. He sees a vine spring from his daughter, which overshadows all of Asia. He sends for the Magi to interpret, and they tell him that Mandane will have a son who will reign in his stead. Having sons of his own, and fearing for the succession, he sends for Mandane, and, when her child is born, gives it to Harpagus, one of his courtiers, to be slain. The courtier relents, and hands it over to a herdsman, to be exposed to the mountains. The herdsman relents in turn and brings the babe up as his child.

When the boy, who goes by the name of Agradates, is grown, he is at play with the other herdboys, and they choose him for a mimic king. Some he makes his guards, some he bids build houses, some carry his messages. The son of a Mede of rank refuses, and Agradates has him seized by his guards and chastised with the whip. The ancestral instincts of command and discipline are shown early in the lad.

The young gentleman complains to his father, the father of the old king, who of course sends for the herdsman and his boy. The boy answers in a tone so exactly like that in which Xenophon's Cyrus would have answered, that I must believe that both Xenophon's Cyrus and Herodotus's Cyrus (like Xenophon's Socrates and Plato's Socrates) are real pictures of a real character; and that Herodotus's story, though Xenophon says nothing of it, is true.

He has done nothing, the noble boy says, but what was just. He had been chosen king in play because the boys thought him most fit. The boy whom he had chastised was one of those who chose him. All the rest obeyed: but he would not, till at last, he got his due reward. "If I deserve punishment for that," says the boy, "I am ready to submit."

The old king looks keenly and wonderingly at the young king, whose features seem somewhat like his own. Likely enough in those days, when an Iranian noble or prince would have a quite different cast of complexion and face from a Turanian herdsman. A suspicion crosses him, and by threats of torture, he gets the truth from the trembling herdsman.

To the poor wretch's rapture, the old king lets him go unharmed. He has more exquisite revenge to take and sends for Harpagus, who likewise confessed the truth. The wily old tyrant has naught but gentle words. It is best as it is. He has been very sorry himself for the child, and Mandane's reproaches had gone to his heart. "Let Harpagus go home and send his son to be a companion to the new-found prince. Tonight there will be great sacrifices in honor of the child's safety, and Harpagus is to be a guest at the banquet."

Harpagus comes; and after eating his fill, is asked how he likes the king's meat? He gives the usual answer; and a covered basket is put before him, out of which he is to take--in Median fashion--what he likes. He finds in it the head and hands and feet of his son. Like a true Eastern, he shows no signs of horror. The king asks him if he knew what flesh he had been eating. He answers that he knew perfectly. That whatever the king did please him.

Like an Eastern courtier, he knew how to disassemble, but not to forgive, and bided his time. The Magi, to their credit, told Astyages that his dream had been fulfilled, that Cyrus--as we must now call the foundling prince--had fulfilled it by becoming a king in play, and the boy is let go back to his father and his hardy Persian life. But Harpagus does not leave him alone, nor perhaps, do his thoughts. He has wrongs to avenge his grandfather. And it seems not altogether impossible to the young mountaineer.

He has seen enough of Median luxury to despise it and those who indulge in it. He has seen his grandfather with his cheeks rouged, his eyelids stained with antimony, living a womanlike life, shut up from all his subjects in the recesses of a vast seraglio.

He calls together the mountain rulers; makes friends with Tigranes, an Armenian prince, a vassal of the Mede, who has his wrongs likewise to avenge. And the two little armies of foot-soldiers--the Persians had no cavalry--defeat the innumerable horsemen of the Mede, take the old king, keep him in honorable captivity, and so change, one legend says, in a single battle, the fortunes of the whole East.

And then begins that series of conquests of which we know hardly anything, save the fact that they were made. The young mountaineer and his playmates, whom he makes his generals and satraps, sweep onward towards the West, teaching their men the art of riding, till the Persian cavalry becomes more famous than the Median had been. They gather to them, as a snowball gathers in rolling, the picked youth of every tribe whom they overcome. They knit these tribes to them in loyalty and affection by that righteousness--that truthfulness and justice--for which Isaiah in his grandest lyric strains has made them illustrious to all time; which Xenophon has celebrated in like manner in that exquisite book of his--the "Cyropaedia." The great Lydian kingdom of Croesus--Asia Minor as we call it now--goes down before them. Babylon itself goes down, after that world-famed siege which ended in Belshazzar's feast; and when Cyrus died--still in the prime of life, the legends seem to say--he left a coherent and well-organized empire, which stretched from the Mediterranean to Hindostan.

So runs the tale, which to me, I confess, sounds probable and rational enough. It may not do so to you; for it has not too many learned men. They are inclined to "relegate it into the region of myth;" in plain English, to call old Herodotus a liar, or at least a dupe. That means those wise men can have at this distance of more than 2000 years, knowing more about the matter than Herodotus, who lived within 100 years of Cyrus, I for myself cannot discover. And I say this without the least wish to disparage these hypercritical persons. For there are--and more there ought to be, as long as lies and superstitions remain on this earth--a class of thinkers who hold in just suspicion all stories that savor the sensational, the romantic, even the dramatic. They know the terrible uses to which appeals to the fancy and the emotions have been applied, and are still applied to enslave the intellects, the consciences, and the very bodies of men and women. They dread so much from experiencing the abuse of that formula, that "a thing is so beautiful it must be true," that they are inclined to reply: "Rather let us say boldly, it is so beautiful that it cannot be true. Let us mistrust, or even refuse to believe _a priori_, and at first sight, all startling, sensational, even poetic tales, and accept nothing as history, which is not as dull as the ledger of a dry-goods store." But I think that experience, both in nature and in society, is against that ditch-water philosophy. The weather, being governed by laws, ought always to be equable and normal, and yet you have whirlwinds, droughts, and thunderstorms. The share market is governed by laws, and ought to be always equable and normal, and yet you have startling transactions, startling panics, startling disclosures, and a whole sensational romance of commercial crime and folly. Which of us has lived to be fifty years old, without having witnessed in private life sensation tragedies, alas! sometimes too fearful to be told, or at least sensational romances, which we shall take care not to tell because we shall not be believed? Let the ditch-water philosophy say what it will, human life is not a ditch, but a wild and roaring river, flooding its banks, and eating out new channels with many a landslip. It is a strange world, and man, a strange animal, guided, it is true, usually by most common-place motives; but, for that reason, ready and glad at times to escape from them and their dullness and baseness; to give vent, if but for a moment, in wild freedom, to that demoniac element, which, as Goethe says, underlies his nature and all nature; and to prefer for an hour, to the normal and respectable ditch- water, a bottle of champagne or even a carouse on fire-water, let the consequences be what they may.

How else shall we explain such a phenomenon as those old crusades? Were they undertaken for any purpose, commercial or other? Certainly not for lightening an overburdened population. Nay, is not the history of your own Mormons, and their exodus into the far West, one of the most startling instances which the world has seen for several centuries, of the unexpected and incalculable forces which lie hid in a man? Believe me, man's passions, heated to igniting point, rather than his prudence cooled down to the freezing point, are the normal causes of all great human movement. And a truer law of social science than any that political economists are wont to lay down, is that old _Dov‘ e la donna_? of the Italian judge, who used to ask, as a preliminary to every case, civil or criminal, which was brought before him, _Dov’ e la donna_? "Where is the lady?" certain, like a wise old gentleman, that a woman was most probably at the bottom of the matter.

Strangeness? Romance? Did any of you ever read--if you have not you should read--Archbishop Whately's "Historic Doubts about the Emperor Napoleon the First"? Therein the learned and witty Archbishop proved, as early as 1819, by fair use of the criticism of Mr. Hume and the Sceptic School, that the whole history of the great Napoleon ought to be treated by wise men as a myth and a romance, that there is little or no evidence of his having existed at all; and that the story of his strange successes and strange defeats was probably invented by our Government to pander to the vanity of the English nation.

I will say this, which Archbishop Whately, in a late edition, foreshadows, wittily enough--that if one or two thousand years hence, when the history of the late Emperor Napoleon the Third, his rise and fall, shall come to be subjected to critical analysis by future Philistine historians of New Zealand or Australia, it will be proved by them to be utterly mythical, incredible, monstrous--and that all the more, the more the facts remain to puzzle their unimaginative brains. What will they make two thousand years hence, of the landing at Boulogne with the tame eagle? Will, not that, and stranger facts still, but just as true, be relegated to the region of myth, with the dream of Astyages, and the young and princely herdsman playing at a king over his fellow slaves?

But enough of this. To me, these bits of romance often seem the truest, as well as the most important portions of history.

When old Herodotus tells me how, King Astyages having guarded the frontier, Harpagus sent a hunter to young Cyrus with a fresh-killed hare, telling him to open it in private; and how, sewn up in it was the letter, telling him that the time to rebel came, I am inclined to say, That must be true. It is so beneath the dignity of history, so quaint and unexpected, that it is all the more likely _not_ to have been invented.

So with that other story--How young Cyrus, giving out that his grandfather had made him general of the Persians, summoned them all, each man with a sickle in his hand, into a prairie full of thorns, and bade them clear it in one day; and how when they, like loyal men, had finished, he bade them bathe, and next day he took them into a great meadow and feasted them with corn and wine, and all that his father's farm would yield, and asked them which day they liked best; and, when they answered as was to be expected, how he opened his parable and told them, "Choose, then, to work for the Persians like slaves, or to be free with me."

Such a tale sounds to be true. It has the very savor of the parables of the Old Testament; as have, surely, the dreams of the old Sultan, with which the tale begins. Do they not put in mind the dreams of Nebuchadnezzar, in the Book of Daniel?

Such stories are so beautiful that they are very likely to be true. Understand me, I only say likely; the ditch-water view of history is not all wrong. Its advocates are right in saying great historic changes are not produced simply by one great person, by one remarkable event. They have been preparing, perhaps for centuries. They are the result of numberless forces, acting according to laws, which might have been foreseen, and will be foreseen, when the science of History is more perfectly understood.

For instance, Cyrus could not have conquered the Median Empire at a single blow, if first, that empire had not been utterly rotten; and next, if he and his handful of

Persians had not been tempered and sharpened, by long hardihood, to the finest cutting edge.

Yes, there were all the materials for the catastrophe--the cannon, the powder, the shot. But to say that the Persians must have conquered the Medes, even if Cyrus had never lived, is to say, as too many philosophers seem to me to say, that, given cannon, powder, and shot, it will fire itself off someday if we only leave it alone long enough.

It may be so. But our usual experience of Nature and Fact is, that spontaneous combustion is a rare and exceptional phenomenon; that if a cannon is to be fired, someone must arise and pull the trigger. And I believe that in Society and Politics when a great event is ready to be done, someone must come and do it--do it, perhaps, half unwittingly, by some single rash act--like that first fatal shot fired by an electric spark.

But to return to Cyrus and his Persians.

I know not whether the "Cyropaedia" is much read in your schools and universities. But it is one of the books which I should like to see, either in a translation or its own exquisite Greek, in the hands of every young man. It is not all fact. It is but a historic romance. But it is better than history. It is an ideal book, like Sidney's "Arcadia" or Spenser's "Fairy Queen"--the ideal self-education of an ideal hero. And the moral of the book--ponder it well, all young men who have the chance or the hope of exercising authority among your follow-men--the noble and most Christian moral of that heathen book is this: that the path to solid and beneficent influence over our fellow-men lies, not through brute force, not through cupidity, but the highest morality; through justice, truthfulness, humanity, self-denial, modesty, courtesy, and all which makes man or woman lovely in the eyes of mortals or of God.

Yes, the "Cyropaedia" is a noble book, about a noble personage. But I cannot forget that there are nobler words by far concerning that same noble personage, in the magnificent series of Hebrew Lyrics, which begins "Comfort ye, comfort ye, my people, saith the Lord"--in which the inspired poet, watching the rise of Cyrus and his Puritans, and the fall of Babylon, and the idolatries of the East, and the coming deliverance of his countrymen, speaks of the Persian hero in words so grand that they have been often enough applied, and with all fitness, to one greater than Cyrus, and than all men:

Who raised the righteous man from the East,
And called him to attend his steps?
Who subdued nations at his presence,
And gave him dominion over kings?
And made them like the dust before his sword,
And the driven stubble before his bow?
He pursueth them, he passeth in safety,
By a way never trodden before by his feet.
Who hath performed and made these things,
Calling the generations from the beginning?
I, Jehovah, the first and the last, I am the same.

Behold my servant, whom I will uphold;
My chosen, in whom my soul delighteth;
I will make my spirit rest upon him,
And he shall publish judgment to the nations.
He shall not cry aloud, nor clamor,
Nor cause his voice to be heard in the streets.
The bruised reed he shall not break,
And the smoking flax he shall not quench.
He shall publish justice, and establish it.
His force shall not be abated, nor broken,
Until he has firmly seated justice in the earth,

And the distant nations shall wait for his Law.
Thus saith the God, even Jehovah,
Who created the heavens, and stretched them out;
Who spread abroad the earth, and its produce:
I, Jehovah, have called thee for a righteous end,
And I will take hold of thy hand, and preserve thee,
And I will give thee for a covenant to the people,
And for a light to the nations;
To open the eyes of the blind,
To bring the captives out of prison,
And from the dungeon those who dwell in darkness.
I am Jehovah--that is my name;
And my glory will I not give to another,
Nor my praise to the graven idols.

Who saith to Cyrus--Thou art my shepherd,
And he shall fulfill all my pleasure:
Who saith to Jerusalem--Thou shalt be built;
And to the Temple--Thou shalt be founded.
Thus saith Jehovah to his assigned,
To Cyrus whom I hold fast by his right hand,
That I may subdue nations under him,
And lose the loans of kings;
That I may open before him the two-leaved doors,
And the gates shall not be shut;
I will go before thee
And bring the mountains low.
The gates of brass will I break in sunder,
And the bars of iron hew down.
And I will give the treasures of darkness,
And the hoards hid deep in secret places,
That thou mayest know that I am Jehovah.
I have surnamed thee, though thou knowest not me.
I am Jehovah, and none else;

Besides me, there is no God.
I will gird thee, though thou hast not known me,
That they may know from the rising of the sun,
And from the west, that there is none beside me;
I am Jehovah, and none else;
Forming light and creating darkness;
Forming peace, and creating evil.
I, Jehovah, make all these.

This is the Hebrew prophet's conception of the great Puritan of the Old World who went forth with such a commission as this, to destroy the idols of the East, while

The isles saw that, and feared,
And the ends of the earth were afraid;
They drew near, they came together;
Everyone helped his neighbor,
And said to his brother, Be of good courage.
The carver encouraged the smith,
He that smoothed with the hammer
Him that smote on the anvil;
Saying of the solder, It is good;
And fixing the idol with nails, lest it is moved;

But all in vain; for as the poet goes on:

Bel bowed down, and Nebo stooped;
Their idols were upon the cattle,
A burden to the weary beast.
They stoop, they bow down together;
They could not deliver their charge;
Themselves are gone into captivity.

And what, to return, what was the end of the great Cyrus and his empire?

Alas, alas! as with all human glory, the end was not like the beginning.

We are scarcely bound to believe positively the story of how Cyrus made one war too many and was cut off in the Scythian deserts, falling before the arrows of mere savages; and how their queen, Tomyris, poured blood down the throat of the corpse, with the words, "Glut thyself with the gore for which thou hast thirsted." But it may be true--for Xenophon states it expressly, and with detail--that Cyrus, from the very time of his triumph, became an Eastern despot, a sultan or a shah, living apart from his people in mysterious splendor, in the vast fortified palace which he built for himself; and imitating and causing his nobles and satraps to imitate, in all but vice and effeminacy, the very Medes whom he had conquered. And of this, there is no doubt--that his sons and their empire ran rapidly through that same vicious circle of corruption to which all despotisms are doomed, and became within 250 years, even as the Medes, the Chaldeans, the Lydians, whom they had conquered, children no longer of Ahura Mazda, but Ahriman, of darkness and not of light, to be conquered by Alexander and his Greeks even more rapidly and more shamefully than they had conquered the East.

This is the short epic of the Persian Empire, ending, alas! as all human epics are wont to end, sadly, if not shamefully.

But let me ask you, Did I say too much, when I said, that to these Persians we owe that we are here tonight?

I do not say that without them we should not have been here. God, I presume, when He is minded to do anything, has more than one way of doing it.

But that we are now the last link in a chain of causes and effects that reaches as far back as the emigration of the Persians southward from the plateau of Pamir, we cannot doubt.

For see. By the fall of Babylon and its empire the Jews were freed from their captivity--large numbers of them at least--and sent home to their own Jerusalem. What motives prompted Cyrus, and Darius after him, to do that deed?

Those who like to impute the lowest motives may say if they will, that Daniel and the later Isaiah found it politic to worship the rising sun, and flatter the Persian conquerors: and that Cyrus and Darius in turn were glad to see Jerusalem rebuilt, as an impregnable frontier fortress between them and Egypt. Be it so; I, who wish to talk of things noble, pure, lovely, and of good report, would rather point you once more to the magnificent poetry of the later Isaiah which commences at the 40th chapter of the Book of Isaiah and say--There, upon the very face of the document, stands written the fact that the sympathy between the faithful Persian and the faithful Jew--the two puritans of the Old World, the two haters of lies, idolatries, superstitions, was as intense as it ought to have been, as it must have been.

Be that as it may, the return of the Jews to Jerusalem preserved for us the Old Testament, while it restored to them a national center, a sacred city, like that of Delphi to the Greeks, Rome to the Romans, Mecca to the Muslim, loyalty to which prevented they're being utterly absorbed by the more civilized Eastern races among whom they had been scattered abroad as colonies of captives.

Then another, and a seemingly needful link of cause and effect ensued: Alexander of Macedon destroyed the Persian Empire, the East became Greek, and Alexandria, rather than Jerusalem, became the headquarters of Jewish learning. But for that very cause, the Scriptures were not left inaccessible to the mass of mankind, like the old Pehlevi liturgies of the Zend-Avesta, or the old Sanscrit Vedas, in an obsolete and hieratic tongue, but were translated into, and continued in, the then all but world-wide Hellenic speech, which was to the ancient world what French is to the modern.

Then the East became Roman, without losing its Greek speech. And under the wide domination of that later Roman Empire--which had subdued and organized the whole known world, save the Parthian descendants of those old Persians, and our old Teutonic forefathers in their German forests and on their Scandinavian shores--that Divine book was carried far and wide, East and West, and South, from the heart of Abyssinia to the mountains of Armenia, and to the isles of the ocean, beyond Britain itself to Ireland and the Hebrides.

And that book--so strangely coinciding with the old creed of the earlier Persians--that book, long misunderstood, long overlain by the dust, and overgrown by the parasitic fungi of centuries, that book it was which sent to these trans-Atlantic shores the founders of your great nation. That book gave them their instinct of Freedom, tempered by reverence for Law. That book gave them their hatred of idolatry; and made them not only say but act upon their own words, with these old Persians and with the Jewish prophets alike, Sacrifice and burnt offering thou wouldst not; Then said we, Lo, we come. In the volume of the book, it is written of us, that we come to do thy will, O God. Yes, long and fantastic is the chain of causes and effects, which links you here to the old heroes who came down from Central Asia, because the land had grown so wondrous cold, that there were ten months of winter to two of summer; and when simply after warmth and life, and food for them and form flocks, they wandered forth to found and help to found a spiritual kingdom.

And even in their migration, far back in these dim and mystic ages, have we found the earliest link of the long chain? Not so. What if the legend of the change of climate is a dim recollection of an enormous physical fact? What if it, and the gradual depopulation of the whole north of Asia, be owing, as geologists now suspect, to the slow and aging-long rise of the whole of Siberia, thrusting the warm Arctic sea farther and farther to thwart, and placing between it and the Highlands of Thibet an ever-increasing breadth of icy land, destroying animals, and driving whole races southward, in search of the summer and the sun?

What if the cosmic changes in the distribution of land and water, which filled the mouths of the Siberian rivers with frozen rhinoceros and woolly mammoth carcasses, were the first link in the chain that was imaginable to man? And what if those changes were followed by other revolutions that went back and back and on and on into the infinite unknown? Why\snot? For all human destiny are thus such.

bound to God's throne with gold chains.

9 798887 728216

Printed by Libri Plureos GmbH in Hamburg,
Germany